Another Day
of Purpose

21 Day Devotional

A devotional that encourages women to acknowledge, see, pursue and know that purpose is in everything that God puts in our lives every day.

Shana Webster

Illustrated by Deanna McCray

XULON PRESS

Xulon Press
2301 Lucien Way #415
Maitland, FL 32751
407.339.4217
www.xulonpress.com

Paperback ISBN-13: 978-1-66281-305-4
Ebook ISBN-13: 978-1-66281-306-1

Dedication:

This book is dedicated to my sisters, Damonik and Niyah. Understand and know that God loves you, and He has a specific purpose for your life. You, your life, and purpose matter every day on this earth.

Acknowledgements

I would like to first and foremost thank my Lord and Savior, Jesus Christ. Thank you for planting the idea of writing a book in my heart. I am truly grateful to have you in my life. Thank you for giving me purpose everyday.

I would like to thank my family and friends for their encouragement along the way. This was not an easy journey for me, but I made it through because of you.

Table of Contents:

Another Day of Purpose Devotional

*E*very day is another day of purpose. I believe that we all have a purpose on this earth, long-term and in every season, but what about in each day? In today's society, our lives are so focused on our purpose, our purpose, and our purpose (which is not a bad thing), but we tend to forget about the purpose of today. We are always looking to the future for purpose, but what about right now? You cannot forget about the present, because that is when purpose is birthed.

The definition of purpose is "the reason for which something exists or is done, made, used, etc." God has created each and everyone us for a reason. Sometimes, we may not find out the big reason (purpose) until later on in life; and that is okay. Until then, we have to live every day as if it is our last. Life goes by fast; it is short; and, therefore, it is time for us to stop wasting time in our day. When we wake up, God has granted us new mercies every morning (Lam. 3:23, NLT). Know and understand that if God woke you up this morning, He is not finished with you, and you still have dreams to accomplish.

In this devotional, each day, there will be a purpose topic, scripture, a devotional, prayer, and a section to apply to your day. Write down your thoughts and answer the journal questions on how you can "live it out" according to the scripture. I hope and pray that you will find fulfillment and understand that there is purpose in every day. God is calling for you to do something special. Therefore, you have another day of purpose.

"Being confident of this very thing, that He who has begun a good work in you will complete it until the day of Jesus Christ."

Philippians 1:6 (NKJV)

Part 1:

Intention

God is within her,
she will not fail

-Psalm 46:5a (NIV)

Day 1

The purpose of today...
Trust in the Lord.

"Trust in the Lord with all your heart and lean not on your own understanding; in all your ways submit to Him and He will make your paths straight."
Proverbs 3:5-6 (NIV)

Devotional:

God wants you to trust Him today. God wants you to trust Him with your whole being, and with the big and small things of the day. He wants you to understand that you can't always know the answer to every question. Instead of worrying about your situation, trust God and walk in faith. Put whatever you are going through in His hands; surrender it all, and He will show you that He is trustworthy and is taking care of your every need.

I am a runner, and every day before I run, I pray to God. This shows God that I am putting my faith and trust into Him to help me make it through my run, because I cannot run in my own strength. I am also inviting Him into my situation. Every time that I do this, God begins to strengthen me. I have learned that when you trust God, He will wow you and go beyond your expectations, especially when you least expect anything to happen. Not only that, but God is a good Father and He wants what is best for His children. Submitting all your cares and worries over to Jesus will give you peace of mind. Trust God with your life, because He ultimately knows what is best for you and knows the right path that will lead you to your purpose.

Journal:

What does today's scripture mean to you? How are you going to trust God today? What are things that you need to submit to God so that He will make your paths straight?

Live it Out

Prayer:

Father God, thank you for another day of purpose. Lord, I ask that You help me to trust You in all things and situations, big or small. Lord, I surrender my worries over to You. Help me to not lean on my own understanding. I ask that You help me to obey Your word and to trust You with my day-to-day life. You are the leader, and I am the follower. Thank you for being a good Father. In Jesus's name, Amen

Day 2

The purpose of today...
Pray.

"And pray in the Spirit on all occasions with all kinds of prayers and requests. With this in mind, be alert and always keep on praying for all the Lord's people." Ephesians 6:18 (NIV)

Devotional:

Prayer is important especially when it comes to purpose. God wants you to pray everyday; Its one of the ways that we stay in communication with Him. When you pray, talk to God about any and everything that is going on in your life and around you. He wants you to be honest and real with Him. God already knows whats going on, so there is no need to be shameful, or nervous when speaking to Him. One thing I realize during prayer is that I have to give God a chance to speak to me as well. Sometimes we tend to talk to God, but not listen to Him in prayer. I encourage you to silence yourself during your payer time and give God a chance to respond to your heart. He may respond with a spontaneous thought, picture, feeling, or a still small voice. Remember, there is no perfect prayer. Don't think that you have to pray like your pastor or your friend. God wants you to be you. As you pray more, your prayers will develop overtime.

God also wants us to pray for other people. Sometimes, we can be focused on ourselves during prayer that we forget to pray for others. I encourage you to get quiet before God, and wait for Him to tell you who to pray for. Maybe there is a friend or a family member that is going through something. You may not know, but God does. During prayer, if a person's name or picture comes across your mind, you should pray for them. You never know if your prayer is what needs to happen for that person to have a breakthrough. Remember, no prayer is perfect; listen to how the Holy Spirit directs you.

Journal:

What does today's scripture mean to you? What has been on your heart lately? Has God been speaking to you about specific things or people to pray for? If so, journal all of the things that He has placed on your heart and pray about it while journaling.

The purpose of today... Pray.

Live it Out

_____

_____

_____

_____

_____

_____

_____

_____

_____

_____

_____

_____

_____

_____

_____

_____

_____

Prayer:

Father God, thank you for another day of purpose. Lord, I ask that You help me to be aware of what is on my heart, and to take it to You in prayer. Help me to be open and honest with You, no matter how big or small a situation is. Thank you for always being open to listening. Please help me to listen to You speak to me as well. In Jesus's name, Amen.

Day 3

The purpose of today...
Forgive others.

"And whenever you stand praying, if you have anything against anyone, forgive him, that your Father in heaven may also forgive you your trespasses. But if you do not forgive, neither will your Father in heaven forgive your trespasses."
Mark 11: 25-26 (NKJV)

Devotional:

God wants you to forgive others. This is a huge command from God; He wants you to get rid of anything that is not clean on the inside. Unforgiveness makes you dirty, and harboring it in your heart is an open door for sin in your life. God wants to purify your heart. God may have a blessing for you when it comes to your purpose, but He is not able to bless you because you are holding on to the past. If God can forgive you for what you have done, then He wants you to surrender unforgiveness and give it to Him. Forgiveness is not only surrendering, but it could also start with having a conversation with the person that you are upset with, if it's possible to make things right. Even if the person you are speaking with does not accept what you say to him/her, or the conversation doesn't go the way you thought it would, as long as you have made peace with it, then God will honor that.

Forgiveness is for you. Not only should you forgive others, but forgive yourself. Forgive yourself for your past mistakes. As soon as you repent, God forgives and forgets. Don't let the enemy creep into your mind, and have you feeling guilty, shameful or replaying your mistakes. Receive the gift of forgiveness that God gives. Remember, no one on this earth is perfect. We are all flawed people that need help in every area of our life. Today, ask God to help you break the chains that are weighing you down; it starts with forgiveness.

Journal:

What does today's scripture mean to you? Who do you need to forgive? What is holding you back from forgiving that person and surrendering it over to God? If you don't have any unforgiveness in your heart, how can you help a family member or a friend release unforgiveness?

Live it Out

_____

_____

_____

_____

_____

_____

_____

_____

_____

_____

_____

_____

_____

_____

_____

_____

_____

_____

_____

Prayer:

Heavenly Father, thank you for another day of purpose. Father, I ask for Your forgiveness. You have always forgiven me, but this time I want to release to You and forgive (insert name). Lord, please purify and clean my heart so that I don't have any unforgiveness bearing in it. Thank you for forgiving me of my sins. In Jesus's name, Amen.

Day 4

The purpose of today...
Put on the full armor of God.

"Finally, be strong in the Lord
and his mighty power. Put on
the full armor of God so that
you can take your stand against
the devil's schemes."
Ephesians 6:10-11 (NIV)

Devotional:

God wants you to put on the full armor that He has given. Every day will have its challenges, but God has prepared and equipped you to face the challenges of the day. He has prepared you to face the enemy and any strongholds in your life. I encourage you to read all of Ephesians 6:10-18 for the full pieces of armor. To summarize, our armor includes: the belt of truth (what God says about you and your situation in His word); breastplate of righteousness (living upright); the gospel of peace (bringing peace wherever you go); the shield of faith (having faith in all circumstances; unwavering); helmet of salvation (knowing you are a child of God and saved by Jesus Christ); the sword of the Spirit (the Word of God); and praying in the Spirit. See, you are already prepared to conquer anything. I know that it is easier said than done, but you have to be armed in not only the natural realm, but spiritual as well.

Walking in purpose will come with its tests and trials, but remember, you can do all things through Christ who strengthens you (Phil. 4:13). Jesus is there with you every step of the way, but you also have to do your part. No one said this life would be easy, but as a child of God, you will be ready to face any giant that comes your way.

Journal:

What does today's scripture mean to you? What does putting on the full armor of God mean to you? What giants do you face day to day, and how can you use the armor of God to help you conquer those giants?

The purpose of today... Put on the full armor of God.

Live it Out

_____

_____

_____

_____

_____

_____

_____

_____

_____

_____

_____

_____

_____

_____

_____

_____

_____

_____

_____

_____

Prayer:

Heavenly Father, thank you for another day of purpose. Thank you for allowing me to have the privilege of putting the full armor on when I am out in the world. Lord, I ask that when things become challenging, please bring back to my remembrance everything that I have in Christ and how to stand against the enemy's schemes. I know that it won't be easy at times, but I know that with Christ on my side, I can do all things. In Jesus's name, Amen.

Day 5

The purpose of today…
Walk in the Spirit.

"So I say, walk by the Spirit, and you will not gratify the desires of the flesh. For the flesh desires what is contrary to the Spirit, and the Spirit what is contrary to the flesh. They are in conflict with each other, so that you are not to do whatever you want. But if you are led by the Spirit, you are not under the law." Galatians 5:16-18 (NIV)

Devotional:

God is calling you to walk in the Spirit. I encourage you to read all of Galatians 5:13-26. Walking in the Spirit means to yield to the Holy Spirit. The Holy Spirit is always guiding and helping you to go on the right path. The Holy Spirit helps you to be fruitful. If there is an area you need to work on, ask God for wisdom to succeed in that specific area. Ask the Lord to show you how to be more kind toward others or to have self-control. As human beings, we're not always going to get this right. That is why Jesus died on the cross for us. We have grace; unmerited, undeserved favor of God on our side. (Thank you God for grace.) God knows that you will make mistakes; this is why He also gave us the gift of repentance, and a helper along the way, the Holy Spirit.

The opposite of walking in the Spirit is walking in the flesh. This includes, just to name a few: idolatry, witchcraft, jealousy, selfish ambitions, fornication, drunkenness, etc. The fleshly desires I mentioned are not a part of God's spirit but the enemy's. When exercising, you gain muscle; this goes for your spirit as well. You have to work out your spiritual muscles so that your spirit man will become stronger than your flesh. How do you do that? By reading the Word, praying, fasting, worshipping and listening to God in your day-to-day life. This will not come overnight, but when it does come, you can look back over your life and see where God has brought you from to where you are now. That is worth giving God all of the praise.

Journal:

What does today's scripture mean to you? What are some fleshly desires that God is calling you to put off? What areas of your life can the Holy Spirit help you to become more fruitful?

Live it Out

_____

_____

_____

_____

_____

_____

_____

_____

_____

_____

_____

_____

_____

_____

_____

_____

_____

_____

Prayer:

Heavenly Father, thank you for another day of purpose. Lord, I realize that I need to walk more in the Spirit than in my flesh. Help me to gravitate more toward my spiritual desires than my fleshly desires. I pray that my spirit will become stronger than my flesh. In Jesus's name, Amen.

Day 6

The purpose of today …
Share your testimony.

"Therefore, go and make disciples of all nations baptizing them in the name of the Father and of the Son and of the Holy Spirit." Matthew 28:19 (NIV)

Devotional:

If you have ever wondered what your God-given purpose is, well, it's to share the Gospel of Jesus Christ, the Good News; and one way is through your testimony. Your testimony is not only how you came to Christ, but what God has brought you through from your past. Your testimony isn't just one experience, but it is your life. Even if you don't think you have a testimony, think about the trials you've been through and how you've overcame them. I realize that what you experience is not for you to hold onto, but to help other people that have been in the same situation. In 2 Corinthians 1: 3b-4, it says, "The Father of compassion and the God of all comfort, who comforts us in all our troubles, so that we can comfort those in any trouble with the comfort we ourselves receive from God." The events, and trials that you went through in your life, will help others be comforted. God wants to use your story, to help other people; whether it's to help a friend on a random day, or a family member, your story is never too small or too big to help another person in need.

The enemy will try to make you feel ashamed of your past. He has definitely made me feel ashamed, but once I started talking about my past and asked God for forgiveness, I was healed. The Word says, "They triumphed over him by the blood of the Lamb and by the word of their testimony" (Rev. 12:11a). By sharing what you've been through, you are not only helping others but you are helping yourself heal. Remember, your testimony can help expand the Kingdom of God. I want you to know there are specific people that God has assigned for you to help build the kingdom. I encourage you to use today to pray, and seek God and ask Him how He wants to use you for His purposes.

Journal:
What does today's scripture mean to you? What is something that you've been ashamed to talk about and why? Do you have a testimony, or events that happened in your life that you overcame? Write down your testimony or write what God has brought you out of and what you overcame.

Live it Out

_____

_____

_____

_____

_____

_____

_____

_____

_____

_____

_____

_____

_____

_____

Prayer:

Father, thank you so much for another day of purpose. Lord, I ask that You reveal to me what my purpose is and my testimony. I ask for opportunities to share my testimony and the good news of Jesus Christ. In Jesus's name, Amen.

Day 7

The purpose of today ...
Live righteously.

"The wicked man does deceptive work, But he who sows righteousness will have a sure reward."
Proverbs 11:18 (NKJV)

Devotional:

God wants all of His children to live righteously; that means being in right standing with God. He is calling you to bear the fruit of the Spirit (Gal. 5:22-23). He wants you to be guided by the Holy Spirit and to listen to Him in how you should live. The opposite of righteousness is wickedness, and God despises the wicked. Being righteous causes you to die to your flesh daily. Jesus is our example of living righteously. I do want you to remember that you are not perfect and if you mess up, please do not get angry with yourself. You never graduate from this Christian walk, and therefore, you will make mistakes. Eventually, you will learn from them. God sees your efforts, and He will honor them. It is in His Word.

In order to walk in purpose and live righteously, there are going to be some days that you will be tested. Are you going to pass the test? God is looking for daughters that are willing and able to do right in any situation they are in. People may talk about you and may not understand why you always take the high road on things, but it is not meant for them to understand. God sees you and understands. Today, let's start doing what God's Word says and not what the world says. You will then be on the road to walking in your true, God-given purpose.

Journal:

What does today's scripture mean to you? How are you going to live righteously today? What are some things that you struggle with that get in the way of you living a godly life?

Live it Out

_____

_____

_____

_____

_____

_____

_____

_____

_____

_____

_____

_____

_____

_____

_____

_____

_____

Prayer:

Heavenly Father, thank you for another day of purpose. I ask that You help me to walk and live righteously. Help me to be receptive to the Holy Spirit when He guides me. I ask Lord that You sow righteousness in my everyday life so that I can become more and more like Jesus. In Jesus's name, Amen.

PART II:
Aim

Yet in all these things we are more than conquerors through Him who loved us.

Romans 8:28 (NKJV)

$\mathcal{D}ay\ 8$

The purpose of today…
Serve.

"And whatever you do, work at it with all your heart, as working for the Lord, not for human masters, since you know that you will receive an inheritance from the Lord as a reward. It is the Lord Christ you are serving."
Colossians 3:23-24 (NIV)

Devotional:

God's purpose for our lives is to serve. My profession is teaching. During the first stages of the pandemic, I did not feel comfortable teaching online, and I did not want to. It was going way out of my comfort zone to be live on Zoom with my students. I remember one day during prayer, God told me that it is not about me but about others. Ouch. Immediately, I was convicted and repented because I was being selfish. I had to realize that when I work, I am not only serving others, but I am serving and working unto the Lord. Every day, we have to die to our flesh to things that we may not want to do, but it helps build our character.

When you wake up in the morning, instead of dreading the day ahead, be happy that the Lord woke you up. Have joy in serving Him. Once your perspective changes and you see it through the eyes of the Lord, then your day will go smoother; and you will be happier about what you do. You will be ready to take on any challenges that may come your way. So often, we think about ourselves instead of thinking of others. Jesus did not die on the cross for Himself; He died on the cross for you and me. God expects us to be the light of the world; in our case, the lights in our job, our family, and our friends. I understand that it is a huge responsibility but that comes with being a daughter of the Most High God. Whatever your job is, work at it with your heart as working for the Lord, and not humans. God sees your efforts and in due season, you will be rewarded.

Journal:

What does today's scripture mean to you? How can you change your perspective in serving every day, especially at work? Who or where is God calling you to serve in this season?

The purpose of today... Serve.

Live it Out

_____

_____

_____

_____

_____

_____

_____

_____

_____

_____

_____

_____

_____

_____

_____

_____

_____

_____

Prayer:

Heavenly Father, thank you for another day of purpose. Lord, I ask that You help me to have a servant's heart, a heart like Jesus. Help me to die to my flesh daily, and to never forget the needs of others. Remind me that it is not all about me, but about others. I ask that You help me to serve You ultimately. In Jesus's name, Amen.

Day 9

The purpose of today...
Be productive!

"Lazy hands make for poverty,
but diligent hands bring wealth."
Proverbs 10:4 (NIV)

Devotional:

God's wants you to be productive. In order to walk in purpose every day, you have to be productive in all that you do. How can God plant ideas, visons and dreams in you if you're watching Netflix all day? Maybe God has given you a vision, but you haven't worked on it yet. Remember, God can put ideas in your heart, but it is up to you to execute the plan. Faith without works is DEAD (James 2:17).

God is looking for daughters who will rise to the occasion. Our flesh can be so wicked, that sometimes it doesn't want us to do anything. We simply have to deny our flesh so that our spirit will overpower it. Don't miss out on your God- given purpose in this life. Be different from your friends and family. I am not saying live a busy life because God has called us to rest, but what I am saying is that it is time to stop living in fear, because "God has not given us a spirit of fear, but of power and of love and of a sound mind (2 Tim. 1:17). Whatever ideas you are sitting on, it's time to execute them. Sometimes, purpose is found by just living life. Sis, it's time to start living! Turn the TV off, give social media a break today, and start going after your purpose. I want you to remember that it's better to live a life knowing that you've tried than living a life of "what-if's."

Journal:

What does today's scripture mean to you? What ideas, dreams, and visions has God given you? What has been heavy on your heart that the Spirit is telling you to do? What has been holding you back from executing your dreams, plans, and ideas? Why are those things getting in your way?

The purpose of today... Be productive!

Live it Out

_____

_____

_____

_____

_____

_____

_____

_____

_____

_____

_____

_____

_____

_____

_____

_____

_____

_____

Prayer:

Heavenly Father, thank you for another day of purpose. I ask that You help me to be productive today. Bless and strengthen me so that I am able to start the new project that has been on my heart. I need Your wisdom and guidance, to push me forward. You have given me true gifts, talents, and creativity. I am ready to be used by You. I ask, that You help me to die to my flesh on this day, so that I will be productive. In Jesus's name, Amen.

Day 10

The purpose of today ...
Be a good steward

"His lord said to him, 'Well done, good and faithful servant; you were faithful over a few things, I will make you ruler over many things. Enter into the joy of your lord.'" Matthew 25:21 (NKJV)

Devotional:

God is calling you to be a good steward over your money. I encourage you to read the full context of Matthew 25:14-30, but to sum it up: A master gave his servants varying amounts of gold. Two out of the three servants multiplied their bags, and the other servant hid his bag in the dirt. When the master came back, he rewarded the two servants with more, called the third servant lazy, took his bag away from him, and gave his bag to the more diligent worker. With that being said, God wants to see how responsible you are with your money. He wants to see how well you manage your money before He gives you more.

Are you on some kind of a budget to help yourself manage your money properly, or are you just spending it all as soon as you get paid? God will not give you more if you do not steward over what you have first. Be thankful for the daily bread that He has given you and manage that first. God loves you and wants the best for you. He does not want to make you an irresponsible person, giving you way more than you can handle. If you are called to own a business, wanting to own a house, or buy a car, God wants to see how you can handle paying your bills or cleaning your house first before He blesses you with an abundance of more. Be wise with your money. Also, don't forget to give first unto the Lord, tithing ten percent (Mal. 3:10). He will supply you with all of your needs. Trust Him, and you will see.

Journal:

What does today's scripture mean to you? Have you been a good steward over your money? Why or why not? What can you do to help improve that area of your life? Do you include God in your plans when it comes to managing money?

Live it Out

_____

_____

_____

_____

_____

_____

_____

_____

_____

_____

_____

_____

_____

_____

_____

_____

Prayer:

Heavenly Father, thank you for another day of purpose and for giving me another chance to get it right when it comes to stewarding over the money You have given me. Lord, I ask that You help me to manage my money. I want to show You that I am responsible for what You have given me. Please show me areas that I need help in and what to do. In Jesus's name, Amen.

Day 11

The purpose of today ...
Be generous.

"A generous person will prosper; whoever refreshes others will be refreshed."
Proverbs 11:25 (NIV)

Devotional:

God wants all of His children to be generous people. Being generous is not always about money; it is about your time spent with others, especially God, being kind to one another, and helping others. God wants you to help others so that they are able to be generous as well. Think about it. When others are generous to you, you want to reciprocate that same kind of generosity. For example, if you are in the drive thru at Starbucks getting coffee or tea, and the person in front of you pays for your order, you are going to want to "pay it forward" for the person that is behind you, and that person may do the same for the person behind them. This shows how generosity can be contagious. Your heart posture starts to change for the better, and that is what God wants. He wants His people to take care of each other. Once you get in the habit of being generous toward others, your life will start to change tremendously. I am not talking about you being rich and prosperous with money, but rich at heart. God will prosper you beyond your wildest dreams. It's not always about the tangible things, but about your attitude towards people every day.

Being generous at work, home, and in your community is important to God. We are called to be lights in this world. God is looking for people who have hearts for others, and not just for themselves. A part of walking in your purpose is to be generous to other people, especially when it comes to sharing the gospel. Generosity is important to God; therefore, it should be important to you.

Journal:

What does today's scripture mean to you? What does being generous mean to you? Was there a situation in your life where you felt as though you could've been generous and you were not? Thinking about that situation, what could you have done differently? How can you show generosity today?

The purpose of today ... Be generous.

Live it Out

_____

_____

_____

_____

_____

_____

_____

_____

_____

_____

_____

_____

_____

_____

_____

_____

Prayer:

Heavenly Father, thank you for another day of purpose. Thank you for another day to be generous toward others. Lord, I ask that You reveal to me any area of my life where I am not generous. Show me how to be generous toward others. I don't want to be stagnant in my walk; I want to prosper. Help me to see generosity in Your way. In Jesus's name, Amen.

Day 12

The purpose of today ...
Don't give up!

"Let us not become weary in doing good, for at the proper time we will reap a harvest if we do not give up." Galatians 6:9 (NIV)

Devotional:

The scripture for today is a promise from God. God wants you to keep pushing forward through the good and the bad. I know that sometimes it is hard to stay on the right track. No one said that this walk would be easy, but God sees you and He hears your prayers. God maybe calling you to write a book, plan a new business, or even host an event. It may be hard in the midst of writing, and planning, but that is where growth happens. God wants to stretch us all and move us out of our comfort zones. Call on the Holy Spirit to help you get through the day-to-day tasks that you have. If you ask, God will give you supernatural strength to endure the day. The Word says, "Ask and it will be given to you" (Matt. 7:7-8).

God wants you to invite Him into your day. When you're walking in the Spirit, then you are able to accomplish more than you could ever imagine. Start working on that business plan, meal prep for the week, get your body moving with exercising, etc. God gave you a powerful spirit (2 Tim. 1:7). You can accomplish anything. Whatever you sow right now will be reaped in due season. Are you interested in what God has for you? Don't you want to see the fruits of your labor? It starts by getting up and moving. I encourage you to write down everything that you have to complete and set goals for yourself. Goal setting is important when planning. One of my goals was to write this devotional. I was so nervous, but I knew it was God's will for my life in this season of my life. I am a living witness that God is faithful, and He is with you through it all; therefore, don't give up on your God-given dreams.

Journal:

What does today's scripture mean to you? What is something you've been giving up and procrastinating with that you know you should be working on? Why did you give up on the task? Write down all of the things that you need to get finished today, and in general. Make measureable and reasonable goals for yourself.

Live it Out

_____

_____

_____

_____

_____

_____

_____

_____

_____

_____

_____

_____

_____

_____

_____

_____

_____

_____

_____

Prayer:

Heavenly Father, thank you for another day of purpose. Lord, I ask that You help me to not give up on the tasks You have implanted into my heart. Help me to persevere today in all that I have to complete. I pray for a diligent and productive spirit. You have called me to do great works, and so I want to see them come alive, Lord. I need You, God, every day and especially today. In Jesus's name, Amen.

Day 13

The purpose of today …
Be kind/compassionate.

"Therefore, as God's chosen people, holy and dearly loved, clothe yourselves with compassion, kindness, humility, gentleness and patience."
Colossians 3:12 (NIV)

Devotional:

God's wants you to treat others with respect. I know first-hand that sometimes it's hard being the bigger person in situations, but that is what makes you stand out from others. People may not notice how kind and compassionate you are, but God sees you. God sees how others may treat you if you are nothing but nice to them. Continue to walk in humility because God will honor you. You never know what being kind will do for you and for others. God may be preparing you for something huge in another season. Why would He elevate you to your God-given purpose if all you ever do is complain, gossip, hurt others, argue, and become easily angered? Those bad qualities are the opposite of what the scripture says.

We serve a compassionate God. He wants His people to be different: showing others how to be compassionate, kind, humble, gentle, and patient. Sometimes you may have to bite your tongue and not always get the last word. I am not saying to be a pushover, but what I am saying is to always carry yourself respectfully. Set your eyes on Jesus and let Him be the example for your life. Remember, God sees you, and He is preparing you for what is to come. Check your attitude at the door; it is not worth the blessing that is in front of you.

Journal:

What does today's scripture mean to you? How can you show kindness and compassion toward your family, friends, and coworkers? What is something that gets you annoyed quickly, and how can you check yourself at the door before your day starts? What provokes a change in your character, and how can you alter that behavior?

Live it Out

_____

_____

_____

_____

_____

_____

_____

_____

_____

_____

_____

_____

_____

_____

_____

_____

_____

Prayer:

Father God, thank you for another day of purpose. Lord, please help me to be more compassionate and kind towards the people that You put in my life. Help me to understand that my attitude can affect the people I work with, live with, and people who are around me every day. Lead and guide me onto the path of righteousness, and help me to check my attitude at the door. I need Your strength, Lord, to make it through the day. In Jesus's name, Amen.

Day 14

The purpose of today ...
Hold your tongue.

"Death and life are in the power of the tongue, And those who love it will eat its fruit." Proverbs 18:21 (NKJV)

Devotional:

Today, God is calling you to tame your tongue. When you speak, you can either help, or hurt someone. Our tongue can be used for destruction or encouragement. Think about it; in today's world, everyone has opinions and something to say. What if you held your opinion and just listened? It is much wiser to listen than to constantly talk. Nothing is wrong with talking, but when you are gossiping, complaining, speaking badly about someone, and talking when you're angry, that spirit is not of God. God wants us to conduct ourselves with decency. If someone from work is bashing another co-worker, just walk away and keep your mouth shut. Proverbs 15:1 says, "A gentle answer turns away wrath, but a harsh word stirs up anger." If there is a person that is yelling at you, it is not wise to yell back and become aggressive. Try something new and talk to them gently or even walk away from the situation until the person calms down.

Remember, your flesh wants to take over and say all kinds of harsh things to people that make you upset, but sometimes, it is not worth it. How is God going to promote you to where He is calling you to be when all you do is speak death, negativity, and gossip? God wants someone that is going to be an encourager, positive, speaks life into situations and bear fruit in their lives. I encourage you to think before you speak (James 1:19). Remember, hold your tongue; there doesn't need to be a response for everything.

Journal:

What does today's scripture mean to you? In what area of your life is God calling you to hold your tongue? Is there a situation that you find yourself in that makes you gossip or talk bad about other people? How can you prevent yourself from gossip and negative talk? Is there something you need to change in the way that you talk to others?

Live it Out

_____

_____

_____

_____

_____

_____

_____

_____

_____

_____

_____

_____

_____

_____

_____

_____

_____

Prayer:

Heavenly Father, thank you for another day of purpose and for allowing me another chance to tame my tongue. Lord, I need Your help in this area. Please help me to speak life and not death. I want to honor You when I speak to others. I pray for wisdom to know what to say in every situation that I am faced with today. In Jesus's name, Amen.

PART 3:
Purpose

I praise You, for I am fearfully and wonderfully made; Marvelous are Your works, And that my soul knows very well.

-Psalms 139:14 (NKJV)

Day 15

The purpose of today ...
Renew your mind.

"And do not be conformed to this world, but be transformed by the renewing of your mind, that you may prove what is that good and acceptable and perfect will of God."
Romans 12:2 (NKJV)

Devotional:

God's purpose for your life is to renew your mind. In this scripture, God clearly tells us that we should not bow down to this world and its standard way of thinking and living. The scripture is not just about renewing your mind in general, but to renew your mind in every area of your life. This includes your finances, relationships, work, health, spiritual life, etc. The list can keep going. God is calling you to change your mindset on how you view certain areas of your life. Let's stop looking at the world for advice, and let's start looking to the word for advice. When you constantly immerse yourself into the Word, your mindset, your thought process, and your old habits begin to break off, and you start to change. When you get to know more of God and have a relationship with Him, you will start to see His will and why you were put on this earth.

Renewing your mind will not happen overnight; it is a daily process. Please give yourself some grace. If you truly want a change in your life, pursue God relentlessly. He is just waiting for you. I've struggled for about two years with my mind and some of the thoughts that I was thinking. The thoughts literally came out of nowhere every single day. Through changing somethings in my personal life, prayer, fasting, and reading the word, my release came, and God healed me. I encourage you to keep pursuing God, and you will see a change within yourself. God is faithful and He wants the chains to be broken off in your life.

Journal:

What does today's scripture mean to you? In what areas of your life do you need to renew your mind in? How are you going to start this process? Is there something holding you back from pursuing the Father; if so, what is it?

Live it Out

_____

_____

_____

_____

_____

_____

_____

_____

_____

_____

_____

_____

_____

_____

_____

_____

_____

Prayer:

Heavenly Father, thank you for another day of purpose. Lord, help me to be transformed by renewing my mind so that I am able to align with Your good, pleasing, and acceptable will. Father, only You know what is best for me; I don't. I am asking You to come into my life and help me to see things differently. In Jesus's name, Amen.

Day 16

The purpose of today …
Walk in wisdom.

"Be very careful then, how you live- not as unwise but as wise, making the most of every opportunity, because the days are evil. Therefore do not be foolish but understand what the Lord's will is."
Ephesians 5:15-17 (NIV)

Devotional:

God is calling you to walk in His supernatural wisdom every single day of your life, especially today. You need God's wisdom to get through the day. You need God's wisdom when you speak to people at work, home, in your business, and even with your friends. You cannot go through life in your own flesh, because then you will start operating in what the flesh wants and needs. When you have that overflow of wisdom, then you will be walking in the Spirit. God wants to help you out every single day. God is a gentleman, and so you have to invite Him into your situations, and ask Him for wisdom; He will generously give it (James 1:5).

Today, ask God for the spirit of wisdom and revelation so that you may know Him better (Eph. 1:17). Ask God for wisdom in difficult situations and in conversations with people that may happen today. Walking in wisdom will help you walk into your purpose. Besides, you need wisdom to help with your purpose in life. I can remember praying and asking God for wisdom when teaching my students. I was so nervous about this specific math lesson to teach. It was very confusing. As soon as I prayed, and gave it to God, He opened my eyes to ways that I could teach the lesson. There was no need to worry because He had my back all along, and He has yours as well.

Journal:

What does today's scripture mean to you? What does walking in wisdom look like for you in the different areas of your life? Have you asked God for wisdom before? If so, what was it? If not, what is holding you back from asking?

Live it Out

_____

_____

_____

_____

_____

_____

_____

_____

_____

_____

_____

_____

_____

_____

_____

_____

_____

Prayer:

Heavenly Father, thank you for another day of purpose. Lord, I pray that you help me to live carefully, honorably, and with true wisdom. Lord, I ask for wisdom on today. Wisdom in every situation of today. Please give me supernatural wisdom on my job, with my family, and myself so that I am able to encourage others while speaking, and to know and understand the day ahead of me. In Jesus's name, Amen.

Day 17

The purpose of today ...
Rest.

"Come to me, all you who are
weary and burdened, and I will
give you rest. Take my yoke
upon you and learn from me,
for I am gentle and humble in
heart, and you will find rest for
your souls. For my yoke is easy
and my burden is light."
Matthew 11:28-30 (NIV)

Devotional:

God is calling you to REST. Resting is so important. In this busy and chaotic world where everyone and everything is calling for your attention, it can be hard to rest. The reality is, you were not made to be on the go 24/7. Even God took a day of rest (Gen. 2:2-3). It is important to take a day for yourself, and to rest in the Word of God. I remember God specifically telling me to take the week off my second job and to spend more time with Him. I am not saying to take a week off (unless God told you to, as obedience is better than sacrifice; I Sam. 15:22); but what I am saying is that when you take time out for the Lord, He will reveal things to you that you wouldn't have probably known, if you were busy. Sure enough, that is exactly what God did for me. If I had not taken the week off and trusted in Him like He told me to, I would not have known what would be on the other side of my obedience.

When you do not rest, you become weary; your emotions start to get the best of you and your spirit becomes hungry. A part of moving into purpose is learning how to take a break from the world and refresh your soul. There are going to be busy seasons in your life, but you cannot let your pride of not letting go of your work for a day get to you. I encourage you to take a day to rest in the Lord at least once a week, for He is the only one that can properly take care of your mind, body, and spirit.

Journal:

What does today's scripture mean to you? Is God calling you to rest? If so, in what area of your life needs a break and why? What does resting look like for you, and how can you rest in the Lord?

Live it Out

_____

_____

_____

_____

_____

_____

_____

_____

_____

_____

_____

_____

_____

_____

_____

_____

_____

Prayer:

Heavenly Father, thank you for another day of purpose. Lord, thank you for showing me that rest is important and that I need it. Lord, show me how to rest in You; and teach me how to take a break and step away from my daily obligations. I surrender all of my worries and fears of what would happen if I take a break. My life is in Your hands, Lord, and I thank you. In Jesus's name, Amen.

Day 18

The purpose of today ...
Be obedient to God.

"Do not merely listen to the word, and so deceive yourselves. Do what it says."
James 1:22 (NIV)

Devotional:

God is calling you to be obedient today. The definition of obedient is "doing, or willing to do, what you have been told to do by someone in authority." In this case, your authority figure is God. God wants you to be obedient to His Word, and what He has told you to do in this season. I encourage you to not just read God's Word and let that be, but follow it. I believe being obedient shows you honor and respect God, and trust Him with your life. You have to be willing to give up your will for God's perfect and pleasing will. If God told you to make a right, and then you went left, that is not being obedient. That is why it is important to know the voice of God within and for yourself.

Obedience also comes from knowing the voice of God. Rarely will God speak in an audible voice (for some people he does), but He does speak in His Word. When you develop a relationship with God, by reading the Word, praying and worshipping, you will get to know Him more. You will also be able to understand when and how He speaks to you. Sometimes, God may speak to you with a spontaneous thought, an unsettling feeling in your stomach, when you feel peace about a decision that you've made, or a nudge that's prompting you to do something. Whatever it may be, God does speak directly to you. When He speaks, it's your job to obey. Obedience comes with faith. On the other side of obedience could be your blessing. Remember, obedience is better than sacrifice (I Sam.15:22).

Journal:

What does today's scripture mean to you? How does God want you to obey Him specifically in your life? Is there something that God told you to do that you are questioning or afraid to do? Are you hearing the voice of God? If not, what could you do to start learning God's voice?

Live it Out

_____

_____

_____

_____

_____

_____

_____

_____

_____

_____

_____

_____

_____

_____

Prayer:

Heavenly Father, thank you for another day of purpose. Father, I thank you for being patient with me, when I fall short and when I am not obedient at times. I repent, Lord. Help me to hear Your voice more clearly, and to not grieve the Holy Spirit when You tell me to do something. I want to obey Your words, Lord, and show You that I trust You with my life. Have Your way today. In Jesus's name, Amen.

Day 19

The purpose of today …
Be still.

He says, "Be still and know that I am God; I will be exalted among the nations, I will be exalted in the earth."
Psalm 46:10 (NIV)

Devotional:

It is important that we are still. In this world, we can become so busy, and it is sad to say but we can forget about God. During the pandemic, I believe that we were put on pause for a reason. I believe that God called us all to be still, and to know He is here. He will get all of the glory, honor, and praise. Sometimes God will interrupt our lives so that we can be still, know that He is God, He is in control, and we are not. Even during prayer, it is important to be still and not constantly talk. This is something that I am still trying to work on. Let God download things in you so that you are able to fulfill what He has for your life. God wants you to talk to Him, but He also wants you to listen to Him as well. Quieting down your mind so that God can reach you is very important. He has so many plans for your life. How is He able to reach you in the midst of your chaos, and busy life?

It is important to set aside time for God every day. Whether it is in the morning or at night, it is crucial that God is the top priority in your life. Sometimes, it is best to turn off your phone, TV, or even the radio in your car and silence yourself so that God is able to talk to you. You never know; the moment when you finally turn off the TV is the time you may actually hear God loud and clear. Remember, being still may take time. Keep going and don't give up. Stillness also means to be patient in the midst of your waiting season and not going ahead of God's timing. God's timing is important; trust Him.

Journal:

What does today's scripture mean to you? How can you make time for God in your life and be still in His presence? What does stillness mean to you? Why do you think it is important to be still?

Live it Out

_____

_____

_____

_____

_____

_____

_____

_____

_____

_____

_____

_____

_____

_____

_____

_____

_____

_____

_____

Prayer:

Heavenly Father, thank you for another day of purpose. Thank you for allowing me to praise Your name and worship You. I pray for stillness, Lord. I want to hear what You have to say to me because that is more important than my busy schedule. Please forgive me, Father, for not putting You first in my life. Help me to spend more time with You daily so that I am spiritually fed, but also forming a relationship with You. In Jesus's name, Amen.

Day 20

The purpose of today...
Surrender.

"For I know the plans I have for you" declares the Lord, "the plans to prosper you and not to harm you, plans to give you hope and a future."
Jeremiah 29:11 (NIV)

Devotional:

Surrender is important to God. Sometimes, you may have to surrender your plans for God's plan because He knows what's best for you. Allow God to use you for His plan. It is still very wise to write down your vision, dreams and goals because God says to do so in His word (Hab. 2:2). However, if YOUR vision does not happen, are you willing to accept that and trust God? Too many times, we make our lists and stick to them; not allowing change to happen. Allow your plans to be disrupted for God because God's plan is the best one. I encourage you to pray and ask God to lead and guide you with a specific idea, or goal that you want to accomplish.

Surrender is a daily act. In different seasons of your life, you may have to surrender your attitude, anxiety, unforgiveness, a person, your way of thinking, or even situations that you can't control, in order to be in alignment with God's will for your life. Sometimes fear can get in the way of our surrender. Don't let the enemy get you to think God's plan is not the right one for you, and you can't handle it. You can handle anything that God gives you. When you surrender, God's desires for your life become the desires of your heart. (Psalm 37:4) Surrendering is an act of obedience, faith and trust. Remember, God is in control. He can do so much when you surrender. He has plans to prosper and not harm, plans to give you hope, and a future; that is a promise from the Lord.

Journal:

What does today's scripture mean to you? What does surrender mean to you? What plans have you written down for your future, and have you submitted those plans to God? Being honest with yourself, are you okay with God changing your plans? Why or why not?

Live it Out

_____

_____

_____

_____

_____

_____

_____

_____

_____

_____

_____

_____

_____

_____

_____

_____

Prayer:

Heavenly Father, thank you for another day of purpose. Thank you for the plans that You have for me, even if I don't know them yet. I trust You, Father, that they will come to pass. In the meantime, help me to become the person that You've made me to be. Lord, I just want what You want for me, and I am satisfied with that. I surrender my plans to You, and I am ready for what You have for me. I give You all the glory, honor, and the praise. In Jesus's name, Amen.

Day 21

The purpose of today ...
Give thanks.

"Rejoice always, pray without ceasing, in everything give thanks; for this is the will of God in Christ Jesus for you."
I Thessalonians 5:16-18 (NKJV)

Devotional:

God wants you to give thanks and praise to Him every day. If you woke up this morning, and your heart is beating, that is all the reason to give God glory, honor, and praise. He is not done with you yet. He has an assignment for your life. He has an assignment for you on today. I understand that some days are easier than others, but don't let the enemy steal your joy. The enemy wants you to be sad and miserable, because he knows that you have a great calling on your life. Try to find enjoyment and appreciate the little things that God has done for you. Just looking outside at the trees, the sky, and the beautiful creation that God has made is worth giving Him praise.

I was once told that there is breakthrough in my praise. Sometimes, you have to just praise your way through a situation and believe that God is going to come through, because He will. It may not be on your time, but God's timing is so perfect. A simple "thank you God" is what He is looking for. When you go through things, your praises get bigger. Don't let the enemy quiet you down. God is looking for your praise because that is His will for your life.

Journal:

What does today's scripture mean to you? What has been holding you back from giving God praise? If praise is what you do every day, then what are the things that you've been praising God for? Write to God all of the things that you are grateful and thankful for. Look around you; that is something to give God praise for.

Live it Out

_____

_____

_____

_____

_____

_____

_____

_____

_____

_____

_____

_____

_____

_____

_____

_____

Prayer:

*Heavenly Father, thank you for another day of purpose. Thank you for every-
thing that You are doing in my life. Lord, please remind me what I should be
grateful and thankful for. Help me to rejoice always, give thanks, and praise You
in everything. In Jesus's name, Amen.*

Salvation Prayer

While reading this devotional, I hope that it has inspired and encouraged you. If you have not accepted Jesus Christ as your Lord and Savior, or know someone that hasn't and would like to, here is a simple prayer that you can pray to the Lord. (I first encourage you to read Romans 6:23, 5:8, 10:9, and 10:13.)

Heavenly Father,

I recognize that I am a sinner. I ask forgiveness of my past sins. Your word says if I confess with my mouth that Jesus is Lord and believe in my heart that You raised Him from the dead, that I would be saved. I believe that Jesus is your son, and that He died on the cross to save my soul.

I ask that Jesus come into my life, to be my Lord and personal Savior. Change me, renew my mind, and make me whole. I ask that the Holy Spirit reveal to me the love of Christ. Have your way in my life, and continue to show me the way to go, and show me how to get there. I thank you for your love, grace and mercy. In Jesus's Name, Amen.

If you have just said that prayer, then I want to congratulate and welcome you into the family of God! Heaven is rejoicing right now at this moment! I encourage you to get into a Bible-believing church and community. Continue to seek God every day, and watch what He does in your life. Remember, everyday that you are on this earth, there is purpose. Keep living, and watch how God moves.

I would really love for you to share your experience from reading the book, and any thoughts from your journal that were revealed to you about your purpose. How are you living with purpose everyday? Is there something that God is calling for you to do in this season of your life? I would love to hear more about your journey. Please reach out to any of my social media accounts below so that I can be able to get to know you better and your purpose journey. I can't wait to hear from you soon!

Shana ☺

Website: www.anotherdayofpurpose.com
Facebook: www.facebook.com/adayofpurpose
Instagram: www.instagram.com/adayofpurpose
Instagram: www.instagram.com/_shana_lw

Citation:

"Purpose." Dictionary.com. Dictionary.com, 2021, https://www.dictionary.com/browse/purpose.

"Obedient." OBEDIENT | definition in the Cambridge English Dictionary, 2021. https://dictionary.cambridge.org/us/dictionary/english/obedient.

CPSIA information can be obtained
at www.ICGtesting.com
Printed in the USA
BVHW081405040521
606414BV00005B/644